THE AUSTRALIAN
Women's Weekly

SUPER
QUINOA

CONTENTS

BREAKFAST

COCONUT & MANGO BREAKFAST BOWL

PREP + COOK TIME 40 MINUTES **SERVES** 4

- **1 cup (200g) white quinoa**
- **1 litre (4 cups) coconut milk**
- **1 cup (250ml) water**
- **⅓ cup (55g) coconut sugar**
- **¼ teaspoon sea salt**
- **¼ cup (25g) finely grated dark chocolate (70% - 85% cocoa solids)**
- **2 tablespoons macadamias, roasted, chopped coarsely**
- **2 tablespoons almonds, roasted, chopped coarsely**
- **2 small mangoes (600g), sliced thinly**
- **¼ cup loosely packed fresh mint leaves**

1 Combine quinoa, coconut milk, the water, half the coconut sugar and the salt in a medium saucepan over high heat; bring to the boil. Reduce heat to low; simmer, covered, for 30 minutes or until quinoa is tender.

2 Serve quinoa mixture topped with remaining coconut sugar, then chocolate, nuts, mango and mint.

tips The quinoa mixture thickens as it cools, so add more coconut milk or water if you wish to thin it down. When mangoes are not in season, use pears, apples or bananas. Use dairy-free chocolate, if you prefer.

QUINOA PORRIDGE WITH FIGS & RASPBERRIES

PREP + COOK TIME 25 MINUTES **SERVES** 4

- 1 cup (200g) white quinoa
- 3 cups (750ml) water
- ½ cup (125ml) soy milk
- 2 tablespoons brown sugar
- 1 teaspoon ground cinnamon
- 2 fresh large figs (160g), cut into wedges
- 150g (4½ ounces) fresh raspberries
- 2 tablespoons honey

1 Rinse quinoa in a sieve under cold running water. Place quinoa and the water in a large saucepan; bring to the boil. Reduce heat to low; cook, covered, for 15 minutes or until quinoa is almost tender and the water is absorbed.
2 Add soy milk, sugar and cinnamon; stir to combine. Cook for 5 minutes or until porridge is tender.
3 Serve porridge topped with figs and raspberries; drizzle with honey.

tips You can use red or black quinoa for a bit of colour; the cooking time will remain the same. You can use your favourite dairy-free milk for this recipe or, if you don't have a dairy allergy, use whichever milk you like.

COCONUT PORRIDGE WITH MAPLE BAKED PEARS

PREP + COOK TIME 40 MINUTES **SERVES** 4

- **2 medium beurre bosc pears (460g), halved**
- **2 tablespoons pure maple syrup**
- **¼ cup (40g) almond kernels, chopped coarsely**
- **2 cups (220g) quinoa flakes**
- **1 litre (4 cups) coconut milk**
- **1 tablespoon brown sugar**
- **2 tablespoons pure maple syrup, extra**
- **⅓ cup (10g) flaked coconut, toasted**

1 Preheat oven to 180°C/350°F. Line an oven tray with baking paper.

2 Place pears on tray; drizzle with maple syrup. Bake for 25 minutes or until pears are golden and tender. Add almonds for the last 5 minutes of pear cooking time.

3 Meanwhile, place quinoa, coconut milk and sugar in a medium saucepan over medium heat; cook, stirring, for 6 minutes or until cooked and creamy.

4 Serve porridge topped with baked pears, almonds and any pan juices; drizzle with extra maple syrup and top with flaked coconut.

tip Quinoa flakes must be fully cooked before eating; make sure they are tender.

APPLE, PECAN & QUINOA BIRCHER MUESLI

PREP TIME 15 MINUTES (+ REFRIGERATION) **SERVES** 4

- 1 cup (110g) quinoa flakes
- 1 cup (250ml) water
- 2 medium red-skinned apples (300g)
- ½ cup (140g) yoghurt
- 2 tablespoons agave nectar
- 2 teaspoons vanilla extract
- ⅓ cup (40g) coarsely chopped roasted pecans

1 Combine quinoa and the water in a medium bowl, cover; refrigerate about 1 hour or until quinoa is soft.

2 Coarsely grate apple. Stir apple, yoghurt, nectar and vanilla into quinoa mixture. Sprinkle with nuts, to serve.

tip For a dairy-free option you can use your favourite non-dairy soy or coconut milk yoghurt.

GLUTEN-FREE • SUGAR-FREE • HIGH-FIBRE

13

LUNCH
&DINNER

POACHED CHICKEN, QUINOA & WATERCRESS SALAD

PREP + COOK TIME 30 MINUTES **SERVES** 4

- 500g (1 pound) chicken breast fillets, trimmed, halved horizontally
- 1 cup (200g) tri-coloured quinoa
- 2 cups (500ml) water
- 2 cups (60g) picked watercress sprigs
- 6 trimmed watermelon radishes (90g), sliced thinly
- 1 small avocado (200g), sliced thinly
- ¼ cup (50g) pepitas (pumpkin seeds)

BALSAMIC DRESSING

- ¼ cup (60ml) olive oil
- 1½ tablespoons lemon juice
- 2 teaspoons balsamic vinegar
- 2 teaspoons pure maple syrup
- 2 teaspoons dijon mustard

1 Place chicken in a medium saucepan and cover with water; bring to the boil. Reduce heat to low; simmer, uncovered, for 10 minutes or until cooked. Cool chicken in poaching liquid for 10 minutes; drain, then slice thinly.

2 Meanwhile, rinse quinoa in a sieve under cold running water. Place quinoa and the water in a medium saucepan; bring to the boil. Reduce heat to low; simmer, covered, for 15 minutes or until quinoa is tender. Refresh under cold running water. Drain, pressing quinoa with the back of a spoon to remove as much liquid as possible.

3 Make balsamic dressing.

4 Place chicken and quinoa in a large bowl with remaining ingredients and dressing; toss to combine.

BALSAMIC DRESSING

Stir ingredients in a small jug; season to taste.

tip We used tri-colour quinoa, but you could use white, black or red.

SEARED TUNA & QUINOA NIÇOISE SALAD

PREP + COOK TIME 35 MINUTES **SERVES** 4

- 1½ cups (300g) red quinoa
- 4 eggs, at room temperature (see tip)
- 200g (6½ ounces) green beans, trimmed, halved lengthways
- 2 tablespoons olive oil
- 250g (8 ounces) piece sashimi-grade tuna, skinned
- 2 tablespoons finely chopped fresh flat-leaf parsley
- 1 tablespoon finely chopped fresh chives
- 250g (8 ounces) cherry tomatoes, halved
- ½ cup (60g) pitted kalamata olives, halved
- ½ cup loosely packed fresh flat-leaf parsley leaves, extra

VINAIGRETTE

- 1 tablespoon drained baby capers, rinsed, chopped
- ¼ cup (20g) finely grated parmesan
- ¼ cup (60ml) white wine vinegar
- 2 tablespoons olive oil
- 1 small clove garlic, crushed
- 1 teaspoon dijon mustard
- 1 teaspoon caster (superfine) sugar

1 Rinse quinoa in a sieve under cold running water. Cook quinoa in a large saucepan of boiling water for 12 minutes or until tender; drain. Cool.

2 Meanwhile, cook eggs in a small saucepan of boiling water for 8 minutes until hard-boiled. Drain; cool eggs under cold running water. Peel.

3 Boil, steam or microwave beans until tender; drain. Refresh under cold water; drain.

4 Meanwhile, make vinaigrette.

5 Heat half the oil in a small frying pan over high heat; cook tuna for 1 minute each side or until browned. Slice thinly.

6 Combine parsley and chives in a small bowl. Roll peeled eggs in remaining oil, then herb mixture.

7 Place quinoa and beans in a large bowl with tomatoes, olives, extra parsley and vinaigrette; toss to combine. Serve quinoa salad topped with tuna and eggs.

VINAIGRETTE Combine ingredients in a small bowl; season to taste.

tip You can also place the eggs straight from the fridge into a saucepan of cold water; bring to the boil, then boil for 10 minutes.

BROCCOLI STEAKS WITH QUINOA & RICOTTA

PREP + COOK TIME 20 MINUTES **SERVES** 4

- ½ cup (100g) white quinoa
- 700g (1½ pounds) broccoli, cut into 1cm (½-inch) thick slices
- 2 small zucchini (180g), sliced thinly
- 1 tablespoon olive oil
- 80g (2½ ounces) ricotta, crumbled
- 2 tablespoons natural flaked almonds
- 2 tablespoons dried unsweetened cranberries

LEMON DRESSING

- ¼ cup (60ml) extra virgin olive oil
- 2 tablespoons lemon juice
- 1 teaspoon finely grated lemon rind
- 1 small clove garlic, crushed

1 Preheat oven to 180°C/350°F.

2 Rinse quinoa in a sieve under cold running water; drain well. Spread on an oven tray. Bake for 10 minutes, stirring halfway through, or until toasted and golden. Cool.

3 Combine broccoli, zucchini and oil in a large bowl until vegetables are coated. Cook broccoli on a heated oiled grill plate (or grill or barbecue) over medium-high heat for 3 minutes, each side or until just cooked. Remove from heat; cover to keep warm. Cook zucchini on heated oiled grill plate for 1 minute each side.

4 Make lemon dressing.

5 Arrange vegetables on a serving platter, top with ricotta, quinoa, almonds and cranberries. Serve drizzled with dressing.

LEMON DRESSING Whisk ingredients in a small bowl; season to taste.

tip Add a pinch of crushed chilli flakes to the quinoa for the final minute of baking time.

VEGAN · HIGH-FIBRE · PROTEIN-RICH

MIXED-GRAIN SUSHI SALAD

PREP + COOK TIME 1 HOUR (+ STANDING) **SERVES** 6

- ⅓ cup (100g) brown rice
- ¼ cup (50g) tri-colour quinoa
- ¼ cup (50g) pearl barley
- 2 cups (500ml) water
- ¼ cup (60ml) rice vinegar
- 2 tablespoons caster (superfine) sugar
- ½ teaspoon sea salt flakes
- ¼ cup (35g) sunflower seeds, chopped finely
- 1 medium avocado (250g), sliced thinly
- 1 teaspoon lemon juice
- 200g (6½ ounces) marinated tofu, chopped coarsely
- 2 sheets toasted seaweed (nori), sliced thinly

PICKLED CUCUMBER

- 2 lebanese cucumbers (260g), peeled, sliced thinly lengthways
- 2 tablespoons rice vinegar
- 1 tablespoon caster (superfine) sugar
- 1 clove garlic, sliced thinly

1 Bring rice, quinoa, barley and the water to the boil in a medium saucepan. Reduce heat; simmer, covered, for 30 minutes or until water is absorbed. Remove from heat; stand, covered, for 10 minutes.
2 Meanwhile, combine vinegar, sugar and salt in a small bowl. Place rice mixture and seeds in a large, wide, stainless steel bowl. Using a plastic spatula, repeatedly slice through rice mixture at an angle to separate grains, gradually pouring in vinegar mixture. Stand for 10 minutes to cool.
3 Make pickled cucumber.
4 Combine avocado and juice in a small bowl.
5 Divide rice mixture among serving bowls. Serve topped with tofu, avocado, nori and pickled cucumber.

PICKLED CUCUMBER

Combine ingredients in a medium bowl; stand for 5 minutes. Drain.

tip You could make a thin egg omelette and serve it instead of the tofu, if you prefer.

serving suggestion Serve with wasabi and soy sauce.

23

SMOKED TUNA, BROCCOLINI & QUINOA SALAD

PREP + COOK TIME 40 MINUTES **SERVES** 4

- ½ cup (100g) red quinoa
- 1 litre (4 cups) water
- 1 red shallot (25g), sliced thinly
- 1 small red capsicum (bell pepper) (150g)
- 1 small yellow capsicum (bell pepper) (150g)
- olive oil cooking spray
- 350g (11 ounces) broccolini
- 2 x 125g (4-ounce) cans smoked tuna in olive oil, drained
- ½ cup (50g) walnuts, roasted
- ⅓ cup fresh flat-leaf parsley leaves

DRESSING

- ⅓ cup (80ml) olive oil
- ¼ cup (60ml) lemon juice
- 1 clove garlic, crushed

1 Rinse quinoa in a sieve under cold running water. Place quinoa and the water in a medium saucepan; bring to the boil. Reduce heat to low; cook, covered, for 15 minutes or until quinoa is tender. Drain.

2 Meanwhile, make dressing.

3 Place quinoa in a medium bowl with shallot and half the dressing; toss to combine. Season to taste.

4 Quarter capsicums; discard seeds and membranes. Cut each piece of capsicum in half lengthways. Spray capsicum and broccolini with oil; cook, on a heated oiled grill plate (or grill or barbecue) over medium-high heat for 5 minutes each side or until cooked through.

5 Serve quinoa mixture topped with capsicum, broccolini, tuna, walnuts and parsley; drizzle with remaining dressing.

DRESSING Place ingredients in a screw-top jar; shake well.

tip Use a lemon-infused olive oil for added flavour and richness.

QUINOA & CAULIFLOWER COUSCOUS

PREP + COOK TIME 45 MINUTES **SERVES** 4

- ¾ cup (150g) red quinoa
- 1½ cups (375ml) water
- 1 medium cauliflower (1.25kg), trimmed
- 1 tablespoon extra virgin olive oil
- 1 large brown onion (200g), chopped finely
- 2 teaspoons ground cumin
- ½ cup (80g) coarsely chopped roasted pistachios
- 1 tablespoon dried currants
- 2 teaspoons finely chopped preserved lemon rind
- ¼ cup (60ml) lemon juice
- ¼ cup (60ml) extra virgin olive oil, extra
- 1 cup coarsely chopped fresh flat-leaf parsley
- 150g (4½ ounces) fetta, crumbled
- 1 small pomegranate (250g), seeds removed (see tips)

1 Rinse quinoa in a sieve under cold running water. Place quinoa and the water in a medium saucepan; bring to the boil. Reduce heat to low; cook, covered, for 12 minutes or until the water is absorbed and quinoa is tender. Season.

2 Meanwhile, cut cauliflower into florets; process, in batches, until very finely chopped.

3 Heat oil in a medium frying pan over high heat. Add onion, reduce heat to low; cook, stirring occasionally, for 10 minutes or until caramelised. Stir in cumin, then add cauliflower. Increase heat to medium; cook, stirring occasionally, for 6 minutes or until cauliflower is tender. Remove pan from heat; season.

4 Add quinoa to pan with remaining ingredients; stir to combine. Season to taste.

tips To remove pomegranate seeds, cut a pomegranate in half crossways; hold it, cut-side down, in the palm of your hand over a bowl, then hit the outside firmly with a wooden spoon. The seeds should fall out easily; discard any white pith that falls out with them. Pomegranate seeds will keep in the fridge for up to a week. Fresh pomegranate seeds can sometimes be found in the fridge section of supermarkets and good greengrocers; you will need ½ cup (75g) for this recipe.

SALMON & QUINOA KOFTA WITH HERB TOMATO SALAD

PREP + COOK TIME 45 MINUTES (+ COOLING) **SERVES** 4

- ½ cup (100g) red quinoa
- 1 cup (250ml) water
- 600g (1¼ pounds) salmon fillets, skin and bones removed, chopped coarsely
- 1 medium brown onion (150g), grated coarsely
- 2 teaspoons ground cumin
- 1 teaspoon ground coriander
- 1 teaspoon ground cinnamon
- 1 teaspoon ground allspice
- 1 tablespoon olive oil

HERB TOMATO SALAD

- 500g (1 pound) mixed cherry tomatoes, sliced thickly
- 1 medium red onion (170g), sliced thinly
- ½ cup loosely packed fresh flat-leaf parsley leaves
- ½ cup loosely packed fresh mint leaves
- 2 tablespoons pomegranate molasses
- 2 tablespoons olive oil

1 Rinse quinoa in a sieve under cold running water. Place quinoa and the water in a medium saucepan; bring to the boil. Reduce heat to low; cook, covered, for 15 minutes or until quinoa is tender. Cool.

2 Meanwhile, make herb tomato salad.

3 Blend or process salmon until finely chopped; transfer to a medium bowl. Add quinoa, onion and spices; season, stir to combine. Shape mixture into 12 oval shapes.

4 Heat oil in a large frying pan over medium heat; cook kofta, in two batches, turning, for 3 minutes or until golden brown and just cooked through. Remove from pan, cover; rest for 5 minutes.

5 Serve kofta with herb tomato salad.

HERB TOMATO SALAD

Place tomatoes, onion and herbs in a large bowl with combined pomegranate molasses and oil; toss to combine, season to taste.

tip We used red quinoa in this recipe, but you could use white or tri-coloured quinoa, if you prefer.

MOROCCAN CHICKEN QUINOA SALAD

PREP + COOK TIME 30 MINUTES **SERVES** 4

- 1 cup (200g) white quinoa
- 2 cups (500ml) water
- 2 tablespoons olive oil
- 1 clove garlic, crushed
- 1 medium red onion (170g), cut into thin wedges
- 1½ teaspoons ground ginger
- 1½ teaspoons ground cinnamon
- 1½ teaspoons ground turmeric
- 500g (1 pound) shredded cooked chicken
- ½ cup (60g) pitted sicilian olives, halved
- ½ cup loosely packed fresh flat-leaf parsley leaves
- 1 tablespoon lemon juice
- 1 tablespoon finely sliced preserved lemon rind

1 Rinse quinoa in a sieve under cold running water. Place quinoa and the water in a medium saucepan; bring to the boil. Reduce heat to low; cook, covered, for 15 minutes or until quinoa is tender. Drain; cool slightly. Transfer to a large bowl.

2 Heat oil in a small frying pan over medium-high heat; cook garlic, onion and spices, stirring, for 8 minutes or until onion is soft.

3 Add onion mixture to quinoa with chicken, olives, parsley, juice and preserved lemon; toss gently to combine. Season to taste.

31

QUINOA & SEED CHEESE DAMPER

PREP + COOK TIME 1 HOUR 10 MINUTES (+ STANDING) **MAKES** 12 SLICES

- ¼ cup (50g) red quinoa
- ½ cup (125ml) boiling water
- 3 cups (450g) self-raising flour
- 2 teaspoons sea salt
- 40g (1½ ounces) butter, chopped
- ¼ cup (50g) roasted buckwheat
- 2 tablespoons linseeds
- 2 tablespoons pepitas (pumpkin seeds)
- ¾ cup (90g) grated vintage cheddar
- ½ cup (125ml) milk
- ¾ cup (180ml) water, approximately

1 Place quinoa in a small heatproof bowl; cover with the boiling water. Stand 20 minutes. Drain well.

2 Preheat oven to 180°C/350°F. Flour a large oven tray.

3 Place flour and salt in a large bowl; rub in butter. Stir in quinoa, buckwheat, linseeds, pepitas and cheddar. Stir in milk and enough of the water to mix to a soft dough. Knead dough on a floured surface until smooth.

4 Place dough on the tray; press into a 16cm (6½-inch) round. Brush with a little extra water or milk; sprinkle with a little extra flour. Cut a 1cm (½-inch) deep cross in top of dough.

5 Bake damper for 50 minutes or until golden brown and damper sounds hollow when tapped on the base.

tip Damper is best made on the day of serving, or reheat, wrapped in foil, in oven 15 minutes or until warmed through.

serving suggestion Butter and golden syrup or serve with soup.

HIGH-FIBRE • PROTEIN-RICH •

LAMB & QUINOA PIZZETTAS

PREP + COOK TIME 55 MINUTES (+ REFRIGERATION) **SERVES** 4

- 1 teaspoon ground sumac
- 1 clove garlic, crushed
- 1 tablespoon olive oil
- 3 lamb fillets (300g)
- 1 tablespoon white quinoa
- ⅓ cup (80ml) water
- ½ cup (140g) greek-style yoghurt
- 1 tablespoon lemon juice
- ¼ cup coarsely chopped fresh flat-leaf parsley
- ½ cup (70g) roasted unsalted pistachios, chopped finely
- ½ cup (60g) pitted green olives, chopped finely
- 1 fresh long green chilli, chopped finely
- 2 teaspoons finely grated lemon rind
- 2 tablespoons olive oil, extra
- 4 pitta pocket breads (300g)
- ¾ cup (60g) coarsely grated pecorino cheese

1 Combine sumac, garlic and oil in a medium bowl; add lamb, turn to coat. Cover; refrigerate 30 minutes.

2 Meanwhile, place quinoa and the water in a small saucepan; bring to the boil. Reduce heat; simmer, covered, for 12 minutes or until water is absorbed and quinoa is tender.

3 Combine yoghurt, juice and 1 tablespoon of the parsley in a small bowl.

4 Combine quinoa, pistachios, olives, chilli, rind, extra oil and remaining parsley in a small bowl; season to taste.

5 Preheat oven to 220°C/425°F.

6 Place bread on an oiled wire rack over an oven tray; sprinkle with cheese. Bake for 10 minutes or until the breads are browned and crisp.

7 Meanwhile, cook lamb on a heated oiled grill plate (or barbecue or grill), over medium high heat, turning, for 5 minutes or until cooked to your liking. Remove from heat; rest, covered, for 5 minutes, then slice thinly.

8 Serve pizzettas topped with quinoa mixture and lamb; drizzle with yoghurt mixture.

tip Sumac is a deep red or purple spice ground from berries. It is used in Middle Eastern dishes to add a lemony taste to salads or meat.

QUINOA, ZUCCHINI & FETTA SALAD

PREP + COOK TIME 35 MINUTES **SERVES** 4

- ¾ cup (150g) white quinoa
- 1½ cups (375ml) water
- ½ cup (70g) hazelnuts
- 2 medium zucchini (240g), cut into long thin strips
- 250g (8 ounces) mixed cherry tomatoes, halved
- ½ small red onion (50g), sliced thinly
- 100g (3 ounces) fetta, crumbled
- 1 cup loosely packed fresh small basil leaves
- 2 tablespoons extra virgin olive oil
- 1 tablespoon red wine vinegar

1 Rinse quinoa in a sieve under cold running water. Place quinoa and the water in a medium saucepan; bring to the boil. Reduce heat; simmer, covered, for 15 minutes or until water is absorbed and quinoa is tender. Transfer to a large serving bowl to cool.

2 Meanwhile, roast hazelnuts in a medium frying pan over medium heat for 4 minutes or until golden. Rub hot hazelnuts in a clean tea towel to remove most of the skin; discard skin. Coarsely chop nuts.

3 Add nuts to quinoa in bowl with zucchini, tomatoes, onion, half the fetta and half the basil. Drizzle with combined oil and vinegar; toss gently to combine. Season to taste. Serve topped with remaining fetta and remaining basil, sprinkled with pepper.

tip Use a julienne peeler, mandoline or V-slicer to cut the zucchini into long thin strips, or coarsely grate it instead, if you prefer.

serving suggestion Serve with steamed asparagus and crusty bread.

SKEWERED PRAWNS WITH BLACK QUINOA & WILD RICE SALAD

PREP + COOK TIME 45 MINUTES (+ REFRIGERATION) **SERVES** 4

- **2 tablespoons lime juice**
- **2 tablespoons olive oil**
- **2 fresh long red chillies, seeds removed, chopped finely**
- **1 clove garlic, crushed**
- **24 large uncooked king prawns (shrimp), peeled, deveined, tails intact**
- **½ cup (100g) black quinoa**
- **¼ cup (50g) wild rice**
- **1 lebanese cucumber (130g), chopped finely**
- **1 medium red capsicum (bell pepper) (200g), chopped finely**
- **¼ cup coarsely chopped fresh flat-leaf parsley**
- **2 tablespoons dried currants**
- **¼ cup (60ml) extra virgin olive oil**
- **1 tablespoon sherry vinegar**

1 Combine juice, olive oil, chilli and garlic in a medium bowl. Add prawns; toss to coat prawns in marinade. Cover; refrigerate for 20 minutes.

2 Meanwhile, rinse quinoa in a sieve under cold running water. Bring two saucepans of water to the boil; add quinoa to one and wild rice to the other. Cook quinoa for 10 minutes or until tender; drain. Cook wild rice for 25 minutes or until grains start to split; drain. Combine quinoa, wild rice and remaining ingredients in a large bowl. Season to taste.

3 Heat a grill plate (or barbecue or grill) to medium.

4 Skewer three prawns onto each skewer. Cook skewers on grill plate for 2 minutes each side or until just cooked through. Serve with the black quinoa and wild rice salad.

tip You will need eight small bamboo skewers for this recipe.

serving suggestion Serve with lime wedges.

GINGER-CHILLI PRAWN QUINOA 'FRIED RICE'

PREP + COOK TIME 35 MINUTES (+ REFRIGERATION) **SERVES** 4

You will need to start this recipe the day before (see tip).

- 1 cup (200g) white quinoa
- 2 teaspoons peanut oil
- 2 teaspoons sesame oil
- 1kg (2 pounds) uncooked medium king prawns (shrimp), peeled, deveined, tails intact
- 2 cloves garlic, sliced thinly
- 20g (¾-ounce) piece fresh ginger, cut into matchsticks
- 1 fresh long red chilli, sliced thinly
- 4 green onions (scallions), sliced thinly
- ¾ cup (90g) frozen baby peas
- 2 tablespoons kecap manis
- ½ cup loosely packed fresh coriander (cilantro) leaves

1 Rinse quinoa in a sieve under cold running water. Cook quinoa in a large saucepan of boiling water for 12 minutes or until tender; drain. Spread quinoa on an oven tray. Refrigerate, uncovered, overnight.

2 Heat oils in a wok over high heat; stir-fry prawns for 1 minute or until almost cooked through. Add garlic, ginger and half the chilli; stir-fry for 1 minute or until fragrant. Add green onion and peas; stir-fry for 1 minute or until heated through.

3 Add quinoa and kecap manis; stir-fry for 1 minute or until heated through. Serve the 'fried rice' topped with coriander and remaining chilli.

tip If you are short on time, cook quinoa on the day of serving, spread it over a tray and place in the freezer for 15 minutes, then continue with the recipe.

MUSHROOM, CAVOLO NERO & QUINOA RISOTTO

PREP + COOK TIME 40 MINUTES **SERVES** 4

- 20g (¾ ounce) dried porcini mushrooms
- ½ cup (125ml) boiling water
- 1 tablespoon olive oil
- 1 medium brown onion (150g), chopped finely
- 2 flat mushrooms (160g), chopped coarsely
- 200g (6½ ounces) swiss brown mushrooms, sliced thinly
- 2 cloves garlic, crushed
- 1 cup (200g) white quinoa, rinsed, drained
- 1.25 litres (5 cups) gluten-free vegetable stock
- 2 sprigs fresh thyme
- 200g (6½ ounces) cavolo nero, sliced thinly
- ⅔ cup (50g) finely grated parmesan

1 Place porcini mushrooms in a heatproof bowl; cover with the boiling water. Stand for 5 minutes.

2 Meanwhile, heat oil in a medium frying pan over medium heat; cook onion, stirring, for 3 minutes or until soft. Add flat and swiss brown mushrooms; cook, stirring, for 3 minutes or until browned and tender. Add garlic; cook, stirring, for 1 minute or until fragrant.

3 Stir in quinoa, stock and thyme. Remove porcini mushrooms from water (reserve the soaking liquid); chop coarsely. Add porcini mushrooms and soaking liquid to pan. Bring to the boil; simmer, uncovered for 20 minutes until liquid is absorbed and quinoa is tender. Discard thyme.

4 Add cavolo nero; stir until wilted. Remove from heat; stir through half the parmesan.

5 Serve risotto topped with remaining parmesan.

tip Cavolo nero is also known as tuscan cabbage; it is highly nutritious, and is also great to use in soups, salads and stir-fries.

GLUTEN-FREE · EGG-FREE · NUT-FREE

43

GREEN QUINOA WITH SESAME EGGS

PREP + COOK TIME 25 MINUTES **SERVES** 2

- ½ cup (100g) white quinoa
- 1 cup (250g) gluten-free chicken or vegetable stock
- 4 eggs, at room temperature
- 2 teaspoons coconut oil
- 1 small clove garlic, crushed
- 1 fresh small red chilli, chopped finely
- 2 cups (80g) thinly sliced green kale (see tip)
- 2 cups (90g) firmly packed thinly sliced silver beet (swiss chard) (see tip)
- 1 tablespoon lemon juice
- ¼ cup finely chopped fresh flat-leaf parsley
- 1 tablespoon white sesame seeds
- 1 tablespoon black sesame seeds
- 1 teaspoon sea salt flakes

1 Rinse quinoa in a sieve under cold running water. Place quinoa and stock in a medium saucepan; bring to the boil. Reduce heat to low-medium; simmer gently for 15 minutes or until most of the stock is absorbed. Remove from heat; cover, stand 5 minutes.
2 Meanwhile, cook eggs in a small saucepan of boiling water for 5 minutes. Remove immediately from pan; cool under cold running water for 30 seconds. Peel.
3 Heat coconut oil in a medium saucepan over medium heat, add garlic and chilli; cook stirring, for 2 minutes or until fragrant. Add kale and silver beet; stir until wilted. Stir in quinoa and juice; season to taste.

4 Combine parsley, sesame seeds and salt in a small bowl. Roll peeled eggs in parsley mixture. Halve eggs.
5 Serve topped with eggs.

tip You will need half a bunch of kale and half a bunch of silver beet (swiss chard) for this recipe. Wash well before use.

ROAST CORN & QUINOA CHOWDER

PREP + COOK TIME 1 HOUR 30 MINUTES **SERVES** 6

- **4 corn cobs (1.6kg), husks and silks removed**
- **¼ cup (60ml) olive oil**
- **1 large brown onion (200g), chopped finely**
- **1 large potato (300g), chopped coarsely**
- **2 cloves garlic, crushed**
- **1 teaspoon dried chilli flakes**
- **¼ teaspoon smoked paprika**
- **1 litre (4 cups) vegetable stock**
- **½ cup (125ml) pouring cream**
- **⅓ cup (70g) red or white quinoa**
- **¾ cup (180ml) water**
- **⅓ cup loosely packed fresh coriander (cilantro) leaves**

CHICKEN GUACAMOLE

- **⅔ cup (100g) shredded, cooked chicken breast**
- **½ teaspoon smoked paprika**
- **1 medium avocado (250g), chopped coarsely**
- **1 green onion (scallion), sliced thinly**
- **2 tablespoons fresh coriander (cilantro) leaves**
- **2 tablespoons lime juice**

1 Preheat oven to 180°C/350°F. Grease and line an oven tray with baking paper.

2 Place corn on tray, drizzle with 1 tablespoon of the oil; season. Roast corn for 45 minutes, turning occasionally, or until golden and tender. Using a sharp knife, cut kernels from cobs; discard cobs.

3 Heat remaining olive oil in a large saucepan over medium heat; cook corn kernels, onion and potato, covered, for 10 minutes or until onion softens. Add garlic, chilli and paprika; cook, stirring, for 1 minute or until fragrant.

4 Add stock and cream; bring to the boil over high heat.

Reduce heat to medium; cook, covered, for 10 minutes or until potato is tender. Remove from heat; stand 10 minutes. Blend or process half the chowder until almost smooth; return to pan. Season to taste. Stir over heat until hot.

5 Meanwhile, place quinoa and the water in a small saucepan; bring to the boil. Reduce heat to low; cook, covered, for 12 minutes or until tender. Stand, covered, for 10 minutes; fluff with a fork. Stir quinoa through chowder.

6 Make chicken guacamole.

7 Ladle chowder into bowls; top with guacamole and coriander. Serve with crisp tortillas, if you like.

CHICKEN GUACAMOLE
Combine chicken and paprika in a small bowl. Add avocado, green onion, coriander and juice; toss to combine. Season to taste.

CAULIFLOWER, QUINOA & ASPARAGUS BITES

PREP + COOK TIME 50 MINUTES (+ STANDING & COOLING) **MAKES** 12

- **2 tablespoons white quinoa**
- **350g (11 ounces) cauliflower, chopped**
- **300g (9½ ounces) asparagus, trimmed, chopped coarsely**
- **3 eggs, beaten lightly**
- **¼ teaspoon ground nutmeg**
- **½ cup (50g) grated mozzarella**
- **⅓ cup (50g) finely grated parmesan**
- **1 green onion (scallion), sliced thinly**

1 Preheat oven to 180°C/350°F. Grease a 12-hole (⅓ cup/80ml) muffin pan. Cut out twelve 12cm (4¾-inch) squares from baking paper; line holes with squares.

2 Rinse quinoa in a sieve under cold running water. Place quinoa in a small saucepan with ¼ cup (60ml) water; stand for 15 minutes. Place over heat; bring to the boil. Reduce heat; simmer, covered, for 5 minutes or until water is absorbed. Remove from heat; stand 10 minutes. Fluff quinoa with a fork. Cool.

3 Meanwhile, boil, steam or microwave cauliflower and asparagus, separately, until tender; drain. Refresh asparagus in cold water; cool. Reserve asparagus tips.

4 Combine egg, nutmeg, mozzarella, parmesan and green onion in a large bowl. Season. Add cauliflower, asparagus and quinoa; mix well. Spoon mixture evenly into holes. Top with reserved asparagus tips.

5 Bake for 20 minutes or until golden brown. Leave in pan for 5 minutes; transfer to a wire rack to cool.

tip These bites will keep in an airtight container in the fridge for up to 3 days.

PUMPKIN & QUINOA SALAD

PREP + COOK TIME 40 MINUTES **SERVES** 4

- 1kg (2 pounds) jap pumpkin, unpeeled, cut into wedges
- 2 tablespoons olive oil
- 1 cup (200g) red quinoa
- 2 cups (500ml) water
- 2 tablespoons lime juice
- 2 tablespoons fish sauce
- 2 tablespoons brown sugar
- 2 tablespoons peanut oil
- 1 thinly sliced long red chilli
- 2 tablespoons fresh coriander (cilantro) leaves
- ⅓ cup loosely packed fresh thai basil leaves

1 Preheat oven to 200°C/425°F.

2 Toss pumpkin in olive oil on an oven tray; roast for 30 minutes or until tender.

3 Meanwhile, rinse quinoa in a sieve under cold running water. Place quinoa and the water in a medium saucepan; bring to the boil. Reduce heat to low; cook, covered, for 15 minutes or until quinoa is tender. Drain; cool slightly. Transfer to a large bowl.

4 Place juice, sauce, sugar, peanut oil and chilli in a screw-top jar; shake well.

5 Add dressing and pumpkin to quinoa; toss gently to combine. Serve salad topped with coriander and thai basil.

GLUTEN-FREE • HIGH-FIBRE • VITAMIN C-RICH

THE GREEN TURKEY BURGER

PREP + COOK TIME 45 MINUTES (+ STANDING & REFRIGERATION) **MAKES** 6

- ⅓ cup (25g) quinoa flakes
- ¼ cup (60ml) milk
- 1 small zucchini (90g), grated coarsely
- 1 small purple carrot (70g), grated coarsely
- 1 small red onion (100g), grated coarsely
- 400g (12½ ounces) minced (ground) turkey or chicken
- 1 tablespoon finely chopped fresh flat-leaf parsley
- 2 tablespoons olive oil
- 1 small kumara (orange sweet potato) (250g), cut into 1cm (½-inch) thick rounds
- 12 large iceberg lettuce leaves, cut into 10cm (4-inch) rounds
- 1 large tomato (220g), sliced thinly
- 1 small red onion (100g), extra, sliced thinly

GREEN TAHINI

- ¼ cup (70g) tahini
- 2 tablespoons fresh flat-leaf parsley leaves
- 2 tablespoons lemon juice
- 1 tablespoon olive oil
- 1 small clove garlic, crushed

1 Make green tahini.

2 Combine quinoa flakes and milk in a small bowl; stand for 10 minutes.

3 Combine zucchini, carrot, onion, turkey, parsley and quinoa mixture in a medium bowl; season to taste. Using damp hands, shape turkey mixture into six 8cm (3¼-inch) patties; cover, refrigerate for 30 minutes.

4 Heat half the oil in a large non-stick frying pan over low heat; cook kumara, turning, for 8 minutes or until tender.

5 Heat remaining oil over medium heat; cook patties, for 4 minutes each side or until golden and cooked through.

6 Top six lettuce rounds with patties, tomato, extra onion and kumara. Drizzle with green tahini; top with remaining lettuce rounds. Serve immediately.

GREEN TAHINI Process ingredients until smooth; season to taste.

tips You will need about 1 or 2 iceberg lettuce, depending on their size. For a vegetarian option, replace turkey patties with pan-fried haloumi or fried flat mushrooms.

GLUTEN-FREE · EGG-FREE · NUT-FREE

CHICKEN SCHNITZEL WITH CORN & TOMATO SALAD

PREP + COOK TIME 1 HOUR **SERVES** 4

- 2 medium red capsicums (bell peppers) (400g), chopped coarsely
- 200g (6½ ounces) red grape tomatoes
- 1½ tablespoons olive oil
- 2 trimmed corn cobs (500g)
- 4 chicken breast fillets (800g)
- ½ cup (125ml) soy milk
- 2 teaspoons smoked paprika
- 1 cup (100g) quinoa flakes
- 1 tablespoon finely chopped fresh lemon thyme
- vegetable oil, for shallow-frying
- 1 tablespoon red wine vinegar
- 1 teaspoon dijon mustard
- 2 green onions (scallions), sliced thinly
- ½ cup loosely packed fresh coriander (cilantro) leaves

1 Preheat oven to 160°C/325°F.

2 Place capsicum and tomatoes in a medium baking dish; drizzle with 2 teaspoons of the olive oil. Roast for 20 minutes or until tomatoes begin to soften.

3 Meanwhile, cook corn on a heated oiled grill plate (or barbecue or grill), over medium-high heat, turning occasionally, for 15 minutes or until corn is lightly charred and tender. Cool slightly. When cool enough to handle, cut down the cobs with a sharp knife to remove the kernels. Place in a large bowl.

4 Using a sharp knife, cut each chicken breast in half horizontally. Place a chicken half between two pieces of plastic wrap; gently pound with a meat mallet or rolling pin until 1cm (½-inch) thick. Repeat with remaining chicken halves.

5 Combine soy milk and 1 teaspoon of paprika in a medium bowl, season; add chicken, toss to coat.

6 Combine quinoa, thyme and remaining paprika in a shallow bowl. Remove chicken from milk mixture; gently shake off excess, dip into quinoa mixture to coat.

7 Heat enough vegetable oil in a large frying pan to come 2cm (¾-inch) up the side of the pan; cook chicken, in batches, over medium-high heat, for 2 minutes each side or until chicken is golden brown and cooked through. Drain on paper towel.

8 Place vinegar, mustard and remaining olive oil in a screw-top jar; shake well, season to taste.

9 Add capsicum mixture to corn with green onion, coriander and dressing; toss gently to combine. Serve chicken with salad.

QUINOA HALOUMI SALAD

PREP + COOK TIME 20 MINUTES **SERVES** 4

- 1 cup (200g) tri-coloured quinoa
- 2 cups (500ml) water
- 1 clove garlic, crushed
- 2 tablespoons lemon juice
- 2 tablespoons olive oil
- 2 teaspoons ground cumin
- 2 teaspoons ground coriander
- 100g (3 ounces) baby kale leaves
- ¼ cup loosely packed fresh mint leaves
- 250g (8 ounces) haloumi, sliced
- ⅓ cup pomegranate seeds

1 Rinse quinoa in a sieve under cold running water. Place quinoa and the water in a medium saucepan; bring to the boil. Reduce heat to low; cook, covered, for 15 minutes or until quinoa is tender. Drain; cool.

2 Combine garlic, juice, oil and spices in a large bowl. Add quinoa, kale and mint; toss gently to combine. Season.

3 Cook haloumi in an oiled large frying pan over high heat, for 1 minute each side until golden. Serve salad topped with haloumi and pomegranate seeds.

FIVE-GRAIN SALAD

PREP + COOK TIME 45 MINUTES **SERVES** 6

- ⅓ cup (70g) black quinoa
- ⅔ cup (160ml) cold water
- ⅓ cup (65g) couscous
- ⅓ cup (80ml) boiling water
- ⅓ cup (65g) barley
- ⅓ cup (65g) wholegrain greenwheat freekeh
- ⅓ cup (65g) brown rice
- 3 medium oranges (720g)
- 1 medium red apple (150g), unpeeled, sliced thinly
- 1 small red onion (100g), sliced thinly
- 1 cup loosely packed fresh flat-leaf parsley leaves
- ½ cup loosely packed fresh mint leaves
- ⅓ cup (80ml) olive oil
- 200g (6½ ounces) goat's fetta, crumbled
- ½ cup (80g) brazil nuts, chopped coarsely

1 Rinse quinoa in a sieve under cold running water. Place quinoa and the cold water in a small saucepan; bring to the boil. Reduce heat to low; simmer, uncovered, for 15 minutes, stirring occasionally, or until most of the water is absorbed and quinoa is tender. Remove from heat; cover, stand for 5 minutes.

2 Meanwhile, combine couscous with the boiling water in a large heatproof bowl. Cover; stand for 5 minutes or until liquid is absorbed, fluffing couscous with a fork occasionally.

3 Cook barley, freekeh and rice in a large saucepan of boiling water for 25 minutes or until tender. Drain; rinse under cold water, drain well.

4 Remove rind from oranges with a zester (see tips). Cut the top and bottom from each orange. Cut off the white pith, following the curve of the fruit.

Hold fruit over a bowl to catch the juices; cut down both sides of the white membrane to release each segment. Reserve juice.

5 Place all grains, rind and orange segments in a large bowl with apple, onion and herbs; toss to combine. Season.

6 Place oil and 2 tablespoons of the reserved juice in a screw-top jar; shake well. Season.

7 Add dressing to salad with half the fetta; toss gently to combine. Serve salad on a platter topped with brazil nuts and remaining fetta.

tips If you don't have a zester to create thin strips of orange rind, simply peel long, wide pieces of rind from the oranges, without the white pith, then cut them lengthways into thin strips. Five-grain salad can be prepared ahead of time; add dressing just before serving.

CARROT, HARISSA & QUINOA SOUP

PREP + COOK TIME 15 MINUTES **SERVES** 4

- 1 cup (200g) black quinoa
- 2 teaspoons harissa paste
- 1.5 litres (6 cups) gluten-free chicken stock
- 400g (12½ ounces) rainbow baby (dutch) carrots, sliced thinly lengthways
- ⅓ cup loosely packed fresh coriander (cilantro) leaves
- ⅓ cup loosely packed fresh mint leaves

1 Rinse quinoa in a sieve under cold running water. Place harissa and stock in a small saucepan; bring to the boil. Add quinoa; reduce heat to medium-low. Cover, simmer, for 10 minutes or until quinoa is tender. Skim any particles from the surface.

2 Add carrot to pan; simmer, covered, for 3 minutes or until just tender. Season to taste.

3 Serve soup hot, sprinkled with the fresh herbs.

tip Soup can be made up to 2 days ahead. It is also suitable to freeze.

GLUTEN-FREE • LOW CALORIE • PROTEIN-RICH

SALMON & QUINOA SALAD

PREP + COOK TIME 25 MINUTES **SERVES** 4

- 1 cup (200g) white quinoa
- 3 cups (750ml) water
- 200g (6½ ounces) snow peas, trimmed, sliced thinly lengthways
- 1 lebanese cucumber (130g), halved lengthways, sliced thinly crossways
- ½ cup loosely packed fresh small mint leaves
- ¼ cup (60ml) lemon juice
- 2 tablespoons olive oil
- 150g (4½ ounces) hot-smoked salmon, skinned, flaked coarsely
- 1 tablespoon thinly sliced lemon rind (see tips)

1 Rinse quinoa in a sieve under cold running water. Place quinoa and the water in a large saucepan; bring to the boil. Reduce heat to low; cook, covered, for 15 minutes or until quinoa is tender. Refresh under cold running water; drain well.

2 Place snow peas in a heatproof bowl. Cover with boiling water; stand for 2 minutes. Refresh snow peas under cold running water; drain well.

3 Place quinoa and snow peas in a large bowl with cucumber and mint; toss to combine. Season to taste. Add combined juice and oil; toss to coat. Serve salad topped with salmon and rind.

tips Use a zesting tool for the lemon rind. You can use freshly cooked salmon, coarsely flaked smoked trout or smoked chicken for an alternative. Add asparagus and snow pea sprouts for extra crunch, if you like.

QUINOA SALAD WITH HALOUMI & POMEGRANATE

PREP + COOK TIME 25 MINUTES **SERVES** 4

- 1 cup (200g) red quinoa
- 2 cups (500ml) water
- 1 clove garlic, crushed
- 2 tablespoons lemon juice
- 2 teaspoons ground cumin
- 2 teaspoons ground coriander
- ¼ cup (60ml) olive oil
- ½ cup loosely packed fresh mint leaves
- 100g (3 ounces) baby spinach leaves
- ½ cup (75g) sunflower seeds, toasted
- 250g (8 ounces) haloumi, cut into 1cm (½-inch) slices
- ¾ cup (210g) greek-style yoghurt
- ⅓ cup (50g) pomegranate seeds (see tips)

1 Bring quinoa and the water to the boil in a medium saucepan; cook, covered, over low heat for 15 minutes or until tender. Drain; cool slightly.

2 Combine garlic, juice, spices and 1 tablespoon of the oil in a large bowl; season to taste. Add quinoa to bowl with mint, spinach leaves and seeds; toss gently to combine.

3 Heat remaining oil in a large frying pan over high heat; cook haloumi for 1 minute each side or until golden.

4 Serve quinoa salad topped with haloumi, yoghurt and pomegranate seeds.

tips Fresh pomegranate seeds can sometimes be found in the fridge section of supermarkets or good green grocers. If unavailable, cut a whole pomegranate in half crossways; hold it, cut-side down, in the palm of your hand over a bowl, then hit the outside firmly with a wooden spoon. The seeds should fall out easily; discard any white pith that falls out with them. Make sure you cook the haloumi just before serving, as it becomes tough and rubbery on cooling.

CARROT, FETTA & QUINOA TARTS

PREP + COOK TIME 45 MINUTES **SERVES** 8

- **400g (12½ ounces) baby (dutch) carrots, unpeeled**
- **150g (4½ ounces) fresh ricotta**
- **100g (3 ounces) fetta, crumbled**
- **1 clove garlic, crushed**
- **1 egg**
- **¼ teaspoon fennel seeds**
- **¼ teaspoon cumin seeds**
- **¼ cup (20g) finely grated parmesan**
- **2 tablespoons extra virgin olive oil**
- **1 cup (280g) greek-style yoghurt**
- **½ cup snow pea tendrils**

QUINOA DOUGH

- **1⅔ cups (250g) plain (all-purpose) flour**
- **¼ cup (50g) red quinoa**
- **½ teaspoon dried yeast**
- **1 teaspoon flaked sea salt**
- **⅓ cup (80ml) extra virgin olive oil**
- **⅔ cup (160ml) hot water**

1 Make quinoa dough.
2 Preheat oven to 220°C/425°F.
3 Trim carrot-tops, leaving a 2cm (¾-inch) stem attached; reserve a small handful of the tops. Wash carrots and tops well. Finely chop carrot-tops; you'll need 2 tablespoons. Combine chopped carrot-tops with ricotta, fetta, garlic and egg in a medium bowl. Season.
4 Divide the dough in half. Roll out one half of the dough on a piece of lightly floured baking paper into a 12cm x 40cm (4½-inch x 16-inch) oval. Lift paper and dough onto a large oven tray. Repeat with remaining pastry and a second tray.

5 Spread each oval with half the cheese mixture; top with carrots. Sprinkle with seeds and parmesan; drizzle with oil, season.
6 Bake tarts for 25 minutes or until pastry is golden and cooked through. Serve tart slices topped with spoonfuls of yoghurt and snow pea tendrils.

QUINOA DOUGH Place ingredients, except the hot water in a food processor; pulse for a few seconds until combined. With motor operating, add the water; process for 3 minutes until well combined. Form dough into a ball; wrap in plastic wrap. Set aside.

QUINOA, ZUCCHINI & HALOUMI BURGERS

PREP + COOK TIME 45 MINUTES (+ REFRIGERATION) **SERVES** 6

- ½ cup (100g) red quinoa
- 1 cup (250ml) water
- 1 large zucchini (150g), grated coarsely
- 250g (8 ounces) haloumi, grated coarsely
- ⅓ cup coarsely chopped fresh mint
- ⅓ cup finely chopped fresh chives
- 2 eggs, beaten lightly
- 1 cup (150g) plain (all-purpose) flour
- 1 tablespoon olive oil
- 6 sourdough rolls (550g), halved, toasted
- ⅓ cup (95g) tomato kasundi or chutney

- 200g (6½ ounces) vacuum-packed cooked beetroot (beets), sliced
- 300g (9½ ounces) heirloom tomatoes, sliced
- 60g (2 ounces) baby rocket (arugula) leaves
- ½ cup loosely packed fresh mint leaves, extra

1 Rinse quinoa in a sieve under cold running water. Place quinoa and the water in a small saucepan; bring to the boil. Reduce heat to low; simmer gently for 15 minutes or until most of the water is absorbed. Remove from heat; cover, stand for 5 minutes. Transfer to a large bowl; cool.

2 Add zucchini to quinoa with haloumi, chopped mint, chives, egg and ⅔ cup of the flour; season, then mix well. Shape mixture into six patties with damp hands. Place on a plate; refrigerate for 30 minutes.

3 Coat patties in remaining flour. Heat oil in a medium non-stick frying pan over medium heat; cook patties for 4 minutes each side or until golden brown.

4 Top base of rolls with kasundi, patties, beetroot, tomato, rocket and extra mint. Top with bread roll tops.

tip Patties can be prepared a day ahead; keep, covered, in the refrigerator.

TUNA WITH QUINOA TABBOULEH ROLLS

PREP + COOK TIME 25 MINUTES (+ COOLING) **SERVES** 2

- ¼ cup (50g) white quinoa
- ¾ cup (180ml) water
- 1 medium tomato (150g), chopped finely
- 1 green onion (scallion), sliced thinly
- 2 tablespoons chopped fresh flat-leaf parsley
- 2 tablespoons chopped fresh mint
- 1 tablespoon olive oil
- 1½ tablespoons lemon juice
- 95g (3 ounces) canned tuna in oil, drained, flaked
- 2 small gluten-free turkish bread rolls (320g), halved

1 Rinse quinoa in a sieve under cold running water. Place quinoa and the water in a small saucepan; bring to the boil. Reduce heat to low; cook, covered, for 15 minutes or until quinoa is tender. Refresh under cold running water; drain well.
2 Transfer quinoa to a small bowl; add tomato, onion, herbs, oil and juice; toss to combine. Fold tuna through salad; season to taste.
3 Sandwich salad between rolls.

tips Use your favourite brand of gluten-free bread. You can use poached chicken breast or salmon instead of tuna.

71

QUINOA, LENTILS & SEEDS

PREP + COOK TIME 25 MINUTES **SERVES** 4

- 1 cup (200g) tri-coloured quinoa
- 2 cups (500ml) water
- 400g (12½ ounces) canned lentils, drained, rinsed
- 425g (13½ ounces) mixed cherry tomatoes, halved if large
- 1 small red onion (100g), chopped finely
- 2 tablespoons pepitas (pumpkin seeds), toasted
- 2 tablespoons sunflower seeds, toasted
- 2 tablespoons pine nuts, toasted

- ½ cup (80g) dried currants
- ½ cup loosely packed fresh flat-leaf parsley leaves
- ½ cup loosely packed fresh coriander (cilantro) leaves
- 2 tablespoons lemon juice
- 2 tablespoons olive oil
- 100g (3 ounces) fetta, crumbled
- ¼ cup (20g) flaked natural almonds, toasted

1 Rinse quinoa in a sieve under cold running water. Place quinoa and the water in a medium saucepan; bring to the boil. Reduce heat to low; cook, covered, for 15 minutes or until quinoa is tender. Drain; cool slightly. Transfer to a large bowl.

2 Add lentils, tomatoes, onion, pepitas, sunflower seeds, pine nuts, currants and herbs. Drizzle with juice and oil; toss gently to combine. Season. Top with fetta and almonds.

SWEETS

RHUBARB & BERRY CRUMBLES WITH RICOTTA CREAM

PREP + COOK TIME 40 MINUTES **SERVES** 4

- 250g (8 ounces) rhubarb, trimmed, cut into 4cm (1½-inch) lengths
- 2 tablespoons freshly squeezed orange juice
- 1 tablespoon honey
- 250g (8 ounces) mixed frozen berries, halve strawberries if large
- 2 tablespoons traditional rolled oats
- 2 tablespoons quinoa flakes
- 2 tablespoons light brown sugar
- ¼ cup (70g) almond spread

RICOTTA CREAM

- ½ cup (120g) fresh ricotta
- 2 tablespoons milk
- 2 teaspoons honey
- 1 teaspoon finely grated orange rind

1 Preheat oven to 180°C/350°F.
2 Combine rhubarb, juice and honey in a small saucepan; stand for 10 minutes.
3 Bring rhubarb mixture to a simmer; cook, covered, for 2 minutes, or until just starting to soften. Stir in berries. Spoon mixture into four ¾-cup (180ml) ovenproof dishes. Place dishes on an oven tray.
4 Combine oats, quinoa and sugar in a small bowl. Rub in almond spread until mixture resembles coarse crumbs. Sprinkle mixture evenly on fruit.
5 Bake berry crumbles for 20 minutes or until topping is crisp and golden.

6 Meanwhile, make ricotta cream.
7 Serve berry crumbles with ricotta cream.
RICOTTA CREAM Blend or process ingredients until smooth.

tips Almond spread is available at health food stores and most supermarkets. To make your own, blend or process whole roasted almonds to a fine paste, adding salt and maple syrup to taste.

APRICOT & CARDAMOM MUESLI SLICE

PREP + COOK TIME 40 MINUTES **MAKES** 18

- 1 cup (150g) dried apricots
- 2 cups (185g) quinoa flakes
- ½ cup (70g) quinoa flour
- ½ cup (75g) sunflower seeds
- ½ cup (80g) coarsely chopped raw almonds
- 1 teaspoon ground cardamom
- 1 teaspoon gluten-free baking powder
- 1 tablespoon finely grated orange rind
- ⅓ cup (70g) virgin coconut oil
- ⅓ cup (115g) raw honey
- 3 eggs, beaten lightly
- 2 teaspoons vanilla extract
- 2 tablespoons sugar-free apricot jam, melted, strained

1 Preheat oven to 160°C/325°F. Grease a 16cm x 26cm x 4cm (6½-inch x 10½-inch x 1½-inch) slice pan; line base and long sides with baking paper.

2 Roughly chop half the apricots; place in a large bowl. Cut remaining apricots in half lengthways; set aside.

3 Add quinoa flakes and flour, sunflower seeds, almonds, cardamom, baking powder and rind to chopped apricots in bowl; stir to combine.

4 Place coconut oil and honey in a small saucepan over medium heat; bring to the boil, stirring until melted and well combined. Pour hot mixture over dry ingredients, add eggs and vanilla; mix well to combine.

5 Spread mixture into pan; level the mixture with the back of a spoon. Top with apricot halves, pressing down lightly into the mixture.

6 Bake slice for 20 minutes or until golden and a skewer inserted into the centre comes out clean. Brush hot slice with apricot jam; cool in the pan. Cut into pieces to serve.

tip You can use walnuts, pecans, macadamias or cashews instead of almonds, if you like.

BAKED APPLES & RASPBERRIES WITH QUINOA ALMOND CRUMBLE

PREP + COOK TIME 1 HOUR **SERVES** 4

- **4 medium pink lady apples (600g), unpeeled**
- **100g (3 ounces) fresh raspberries**
- **2 teaspoons finely grated lemon rind**
- **1 tablespoon low-GI cane sugar**

CRUMBLE TOPPING

- **2 tablespoons quinoa flakes**
- **1 tablespoon white spelt flour**
- **2 tablespoons coarsely chopped roasted almonds**
- **1 teaspoon low-GI cane sugar**
- **2 teaspoons butter**
- **pinch cinnamon**

1 Preheat oven to 160°C/325°F. Grease and line a baking tray with baking paper.

2 Make crumble topping.

3 Core unpeeled apples about three-quarters of the way down from stem end, making the hole 4cm (1½ inches) in diameter. Use a small sharp knife to score around the centre of each apple. Make a small deep cut in the base of each apple.

4 Pack combined raspberries, rind and sugar firmly into apples; top with crumble topping. Place apples on tray. Bake, uncovered, for 45 minutes or until apples are just tender.

CRUMBLE TOPPING

Place ingredients in a small bowl; using your fingers, rub the mixture together until well combined.

tips Use your favourite variety of apple; we used pink lady as they have a sweet flavour that marries well with the raspberries. If you don't have an apple corer, you can use a melon baller to remove the apple core.

serving suggestion Serve with low-fat ice-cream or yoghurt.

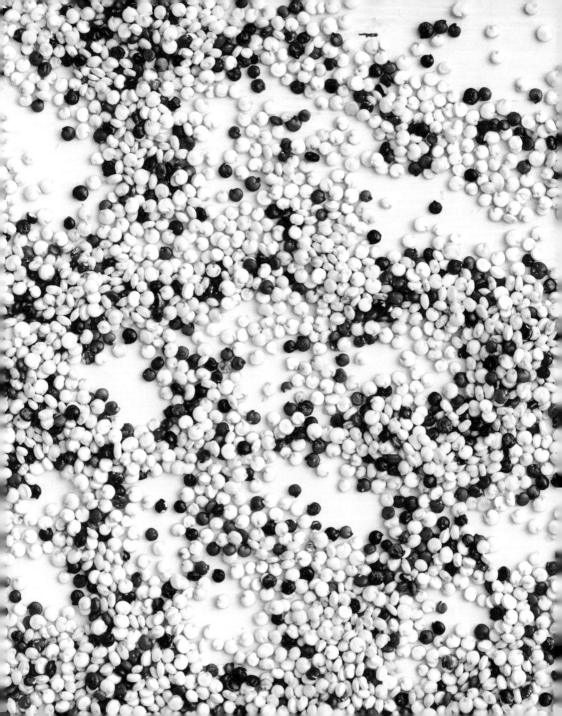

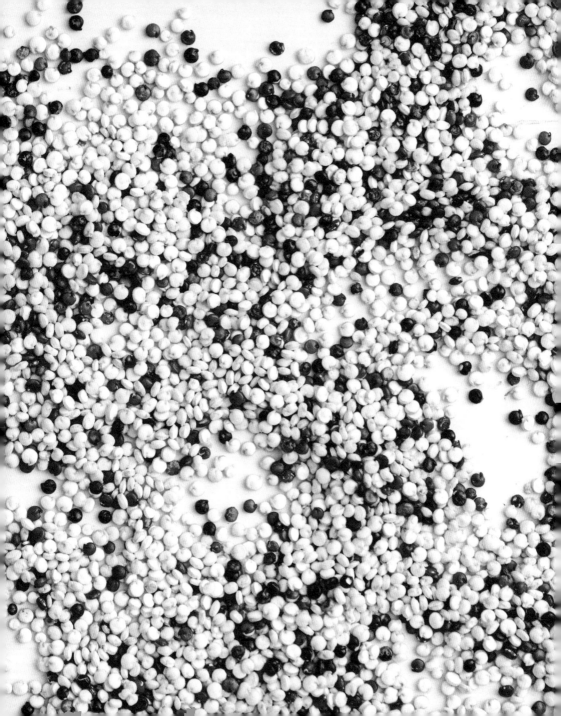

GLOSSARY

AGAVE SYRUP from the agave plant; has a low GI, but that is due to the high percentage of fructose present, which may be harmful in large quantities.

ALLSPICE also known as pimento or jamaican pepper; so-named because it tastes like a combination of nutmeg, cumin, clove and cinnamon. Available whole or ground.

ALMONDS flat, pointy-tipped nuts having a pitted brown shell enclosing a creamy white kernel which is covered by a brown skin.

flaked paper-thin slices.

AVOCADO the fruit of a family of large evergreen trees originating in Central and South America. Ripe avocados have soft, buttery flesh and a nutty flavour, and contain a high level of monounsaturated oil.

BAKING PAPER also known as parchment paper or baking parchment – is a silicone-coated paper that is primarily used for lining baking pans and oven trays so cakes and biscuits won't stick, making removal easy.

BAKING POWDER a raising agent consisting mainly of two parts cream of tartar to one part bicarbonate of soda (baking soda).

BARLEY a nutritious grain used in soups and stews. Hulled barley, the least processed, is high in fibre. Pearl barley has had the husk removed then been steamed and polished so that only the 'pearl' of the original grain remains, much the same as white rice.

BASIL used extensively in Italian dishes and one of the main ingredients in pesto.

BROCCOLINI a cross between broccoli and chinese kale; it has long asparagus-like stems with a long loose floret, both are edible. Resembles broccoli but is milder and sweeter in taste.

BUTTER use salted or unsalted (sweet) butter; 125g (4 ounces) is equal to one stick of butter.

CAPERS grey-green buds of a warm climate shrub (usually Mediterranean), sold either dried and salted or pickled in a vinegar brine. Capers must be rinsed well before using.

CAPSICUM (BELL PEPPER) also called pepper. Comes in many colours: red, green, yellow, orange and purplish-black. Be sure to discard seeds and membranes before use.

CARDAMOM a spice native to India; can be purchased in pod, seed or ground form.

CHEESE

fetta Greek in origin; a crumbly textured goat- or sheep-milk cheese having a sharp, salty taste. Ripened and stored in salted whey.

haloumi a firm, cream-coloured sheep-milk cheese matured in brine; haloumi can be grilled or fried, briefly, without breaking down. Should be eaten while still warm as it becomes tough and rubbery on cooling.

mozzarella a delicate, semi-soft, white cheese traditionally made from buffalo milk. Sold fresh, it spoils rapidly so will only keep, refrigerated in brine, for 1 or 2 days at the most.

parmesan also called parmigiano; is a hard, grainy cow-milk cheese originating in Italy. Reggiano is the best variety.

pecorino hard, white to pale-yellow in colour. If you can't find it, use parmesan instead.

ricotta a soft, sweet, moist, white cow-milk cheese with a low fat content (8.5 %) and a slightly grainy texture. The name roughly translates as "cooked again", referring to ricotta's manufacture from a whey that is itself a by-product of other cheese making.

CHILLI use rubber gloves when seeding and chopping fresh chillies as they can burn your skin.

flakes, dried deep-red, dehydrated chilli slices and whole seeds.

long red available both fresh and dried; a generic term used for any moderately hot, long, thin chilli (about 6cm to 8cm long).

thai (serrano) also known as "scuds"; tiny, very hot and bright red in colour.

CHIVES related to the onion and leek; has a subtle onion flavour.

CHOCOLATE, DARK (SEMI-SWEET) also called luxury chocolate; made of a high percentage of cocoa liquor and cocoa butter, and little added sugar. Dark chocolate is ideal for use in desserts and cakes.

CINNAMON available both in the piece (called sticks or quills) and ground into powder; one of the world's most common spices.

COCONUT

flaked dried flaked coconut flesh.

milk not the liquid inside the fruit (coconut water), but the diluted liquid from the second pressing of the white flesh of a mature coconut. Available in cans and cartons at most supermarkets.

oil is extracted from the coconut flesh so you don't get any of the fibre, protein or carbohydrates present in the whole coconut. The best quality is virgin coconut oil, which is the oil pressed from the dried coconut flesh, and doesn't include the use of solvents or other refining processes.

sugar is not made from coconuts, but from the sap of the blossoms of the coconut palm tree. The refined sap looks a little like raw or light brown sugar, and has a similar caramel flavour. It also has the same amount of kilojoules as regular table (white) sugar.

CORIANDER (CILANTRO) also known as pak chee, cilantro or chinese parsley; bright-green leafy herb with a pungent flavour. Both the stems and roots of coriander are used; wash well before using. Is also available ground or as seeds; these should not be substituted for fresh.

COUSCOUS a fine, grain-like cereal product made from semolina; from the countries of North Africa. A semolina flour and water dough is sieved then dehydrated to produce minuscule even-sized pellets of couscous; when rehydrated it swells to three or four times its original size.

CRANBERRIES, DRIED they have the same slightly sour, succulent flavour as fresh cranberries.

CREAM, POURING also called pure or fresh cream. It has no additives and contains a minimum fat content of 35%.

CUCUMBER, LEBANESE short, slender and thin-skinned. Probably the most popular variety because of its tender, edible skin, tiny, yielding seeds, and sweet, fresh and flavoursome taste.

CUMIN also known as zeera or comino; resembling caraway in size, cumin is the dried seed of a plant related to the parsley family. Black cumin seeds are smaller than standard cumin, and dark brown rather than true black.

CURRANTS tiny, almost black raisins so-named after a grape variety that originated in Corinth, Greece.

EGGS we use large chicken eggs weighing an average of 60g unless stated otherwise in the recipes in this book.

FENNEL also known as finocchio or anise; a white to very pale green-white, firm, crisp, roundish vegetable. The bulb has a slightly sweet, anise flavour but the leaves have a much stronger taste.

FISH SAUCE called nuoc nam (Vietnamese) or nam pla (Thai); made from pulverised salted fermented fish, most often anchovies.

FLOUR

plain (all-purpose) a general all-purpose wheat flour.

self-raising plain flour sifted with baking powder in the proportion of 1 cup flour to 2 teaspoons baking powder.

FREEKEH also known as farek, young green wheat that has been toasted and cracked.

GINGER

fresh also called green or root ginger; thick gnarled root of a tropical plant.

ground also called powdered ginger; used as a flavouring in baking but cannot be substituted for fresh ginger.

HARISSA a Moroccan paste made from dried chillies, cumin, garlic, oil and caraway seeds. Available from Middle Eastern food shops and supermarkets.

HONEY the variety sold in a squeezable container is not suitable for the recipes in this book.

ICEBERG LETTUCE a heavy, firm round lettuce with tightly packed leaves and crisp texture.

KALE is a type of leafy cabbage, rich in nutrients and vitamins. Leaf colours can range from green to violet.

KUMARA (ORANGE SWEET POTATO) the Māori name of an orange-fleshed sweet potato. often confused with yam.

LENTILS (red, brown, yellow) dried pulses often identified by and named after their colour; also known as dhal.

LINSEEDS also known as flaxseeds, they are the richest plant source of omega 3 fats, which are essential for a healthy brain, heart, joints and immune system.

MACADAMIAS native to Australia; fairly large, slightly soft, buttery rich nut. Used to make oil and macadamia butter; equally good in salads or cakes and pastries; delicious eaten on their own. Should always be stored in the fridge to prevent their high oil content turning them rancid.

MAPLE SYRUP, PURE distilled from the sap of sugar maple trees found only in Canada and the USA. Maple-flavoured syrup or pancake syrup is not an adequate substitute for the real thing.

MILK we use full-cream homogenised milk unless otherwise specified.

soy rich creamy 'milk' extracted from soya beans that have been crushed in hot water and strained. It has a nutty flavour.

MUSHROOMS

flat large, flat mushrooms with a rich earthy flavour. They are sometimes misnamed field mushrooms, which are wild mushrooms.

porcini, dried rich-flavoured mushrooms, also known as cèpes. Has a strong nutty flavour, so only small amounts are required. Rehydrate before use.

swiss brown also known as cremini or roman mushrooms; are light brown mushrooms with a full-bodied flavour.

NORI a type of dried seaweed used as a flavouring, garnish or for sushi. Sold in thin sheets, plain or toasted (yaki-nori).

NUTMEG a strong and pungent spice ground from the dried nut of an evergreen tree native to Indonesia. Usually found ground but the flavour is more intense from a whole nut, so it's best to grate your own, available from spice shops.

OIL

coconut see *Coconut*

cooking spray we use a cholesterol-free cooking spray made from canola oil.

olive made from ripened olives; "light" refers to taste not fat levels.

peanut pressed from ground peanuts; commonly used oil in Asian cooking because of its high smoke point (capacity to handle high heat without burning).

sesame made from roasted, crushed, white sesame seeds; a flavouring rather than a cooking medium.

vegetable any of a number of oils sourced from plant rather than animal fats.

ONIONS

green (scallions) also known, incorrectly, as shallots; an immature onion picked before the bulb has formed, having a long, bright-green edible stalk.

red also known as spanish, red spanish or bermuda onion; a sweet-flavoured, large, purple-red onion.

shallots also called french shallots, golden shallots or eschalots. Small and elongated, with a brown skin, they grow in tight clusters similar to garlic.

spring crisp, narrow green-leafed tops and a round sweet white bulb larger than green onions.

PAPRIKA ground, dried, sweet red capsicum (bell pepper); there are many types available, including sweet, hot, mild and smoked.

PECANS native to the US and now grown locally; pecans are golden brown, buttery and rich. Good in savoury as well as sweet dishes; walnuts are a good substitute.

PEPITAS (PUMPKIN SEEDS) are the pale green kernels of dried pumpkin seeds; they can be bought plain or salted.

PINE NUTS also known as pignoli; not a nut but a small, cream-coloured kernel from pine cones. They are best roasted before use to bring out the flavour.

PISTACHIOS green, delicately flavoured nuts inside hard off-white shells. Available salted or unsalted in their shells; you can also get them shelled.

POMEGRANATE dark-red, leathery-skinned fruit about the size of an orange filled with hundreds of seeds, each wrapped in an edible lucent-crimson pulp with a unique tangy sweet-sour flavour.

POMEGRANATE MOLASSES not to be confused with pomegranate syrup or grenadine (used in cocktails); pomegranate molasses is thicker, browner, and more concentrated in flavour — tart and sharp, slightly sweet and fruity. Brush over grilling or roasting meat, seafood or poultry, add to salad dressings or sauces. Buy from Middle Eastern food stores or specialty food shops.

PRESERVED LEMON RIND a North African specialty; lemons are quartered and preserved in salt and lemon juice or water. To use, remove and discard pulp, squeeze juice from rind, rinse rind well; slice thinly. Once opened, store under refrigeration.

QUINOA pronounced keen-wa; is the seed of a leafy plant similar to spinach. It has a delicate, slightly nutty taste and chewy texture.

flakes the grains have been rolled and flattened.

RICE, BROWN retains the high-fibre, nutritious bran coating that's removed from white rice when hulled. It takes longer to cook than white rice and has a chewier texture. Once cooked, the long grains stay separate, while the short grains are soft and stickier.

ROLLED OATS flattened oat grain rolled into flakes and traditionally used for porridge. Instant oats are also available, but use traditional oats for baking.

SESAME SEEDS black and white are the most common of this small oval seed. Roast the seeds in a heavy-based frying pan over low heat.

SILVER BEET also called swiss chard; mistakenly called spinach.

SNOW PEAS also called mangetout; a variety of pea, eaten pod and all (although you may need to string them). Used in stir-fries or eaten raw in salads.

SPINACH also known as english spinach and incorrectly, silver beet. Baby spinach leaves are best eaten raw in salads; the larger leaves should be cooked until barely wilted.

SUGAR

brown very soft, finely granulated sugar retaining molasses for its characteristic colour and flavour.

caster (superfine) finely granulated table sugar.

coconut see *Coconut*

low-gi cane a molasses extract is sprayed onto raw sugar, increasing the time it takes to digest the sugar, resulting in a slower release of energy.

SUMAC a purple-red, astringent spice ground from berries growing on shrubs that flourish wild around the Mediterranean.

SUNFLOWER SEEDS grey-green, slightly soft, oily kernels; a nutritious snack.

TAHINI a rich, sesame-seed paste, used in most Middle-Eastern cuisines, especially Lebanese, in dips and sauces.

TOFU also called bean curd; an off-white, custard-like product made from the "milk" of crushed soybeans. Comes fresh as soft or firm, and processed as fried or pressed dried sheets.

TURMERIC also called kamin; is a rhizome related to galangal and ginger. Known for the golden colour it imparts, fresh turmeric can be substituted with the more commonly found dried powder.

VINEGAR

balsamic originally from Modena, Italy, there are now many balsamic vinegars on the market ranging in pungency and quality depending on how, and for how long, they have been aged.

red wine based on fermented red wine.

rice a colourless vinegar made from fermented rice and flavoured with sugar and salt.

rice wine vinegar made from rice wine lees (sediment left after fermentation), salt and alcohol.

WALNUTS as well as being a good source of fibre and healthy oils, nuts contain a range of vitamins, minerals and other beneficial plant components called phytochemicals. Each type of nut has a special make-up and walnuts contain the beneficial omega-3 fatty acids.

WATERCRESS one of the cress family, a large group of peppery greens. Highly perishable, so must be used as soon as possible after purchase. It has an exceptionally high vitamin K content, which is great for eye health, and is an excellent source of calcium.

YEAST (dried and fresh), a raising agent used in dough making. Granular (7g sachets) and fresh compressed (20g blocks) yeast can almost always be substituted for the other.

YOGHURT, GREEK-STYLE plain yoghurt strained in a cloth (muslin) to remove the whey and to give it a creamy consistency.

ZUCCHINI also called courgette; a small, pale- or dark-green or yellow vegetable belonging to the squash family.

CONVERSION CHART

MEASURES

One Australian metric measuring cup holds approximately 250ml; one Australian metric tablespoon holds 20ml; one Australian metric teaspoon holds 5ml.

The difference between one country's measuring cups and another's is within a two- or three-teaspoon variance, and will not affect your cooking results. North America, New Zealand and the United Kingdom use a 15ml tablespoon.

All cup and spoon measurements are level. The most accurate way of measuring dry ingredients is to weigh them. When measuring liquids, use a clear glass or plastic jug with the metric markings.

The imperial measurements used in these recipes are approximate only. Measurements for cake pans are approximate only. Using same-shaped cake pans of a similar size should not affect the outcome of your baking. We measure the inside top of the cake pan to determine sizes.

We use large eggs with an average weight of 60g.

DRY MEASURES

METRIC	IMPERIAL
15G	½OZ
30G	1OZ
60G	2OZ
90G	3OZ
125G	4OZ (¼LB)
155G	5OZ
185G	6OZ
220G	7OZ
250G	8OZ (½LB)
280G	9OZ
315G	10OZ
345G	11OZ
375G	12OZ (¾LB)
410G	13OZ
440G	14OZ
470G	15OZ
500G	16OZ (1LB)
750G	24OZ (1½LB)
1KG	32OZ (2LB)

LIQUID MEASURES

METRIC	IMPERIAL
30ML	1 FLUID OZ
60ML	2 FLUID OZ
100ML	3 FLUID OZ
125ML	4 FLUID OZ
150ML	5 FLUID OZ
190ML	6 FLUID OZ
250ML	8 FLUID OZ
300ML	10 FLUID OZ
500ML	16 FLUID OZ
600ML	20 FLUID OZ
1000ML (1 LITRE)	1¾ PINTS

LENGTH MEASURES

METRIC	IMPERIAL
3MM	⅛IN
6MM	¼IN
1CM	½IN
2CM	¾IN
2.5CM	1IN
5CM	2IN
6CM	2½IN
8CM	3IN
10CM	4IN
13CM	5IN
15CM	6IN
18CM	7IN
20CM	8IN
22CM	9IN
25CM	10IN
28CM	11IN
30CM	12IN (1FT)

OVEN TEMPERATURES

The oven temperatures in this book are for conventional ovens; if you have a fan-forced oven, decrease the temperature by 10-20 degrees.

	°C (CELSIUS)	°F (FAHRENHEIT)
VERY SLOW	120	250
SLOW	150	300
MODERATELY SLOW	160	325
MODERATE	180	350
MODERATELY HOT	200	400
HOT	220	425
VERY HOT	240	475

INDEX

PUBLISHED IN 2016 BY BAUER MEDIA BOOKS, AUSTRALIA.
BAUER MEDIA BOOKS IS A DIVISION OF BAUER MEDIA PTY LTD.

BAUER MEDIA BOOKS

PUBLISHER
JO RUNCIMAN
EDITORIAL & FOOD DIRECTOR
PAMELA CLARK
DIRECTOR OF SALES, MARKETING & RIGHTS
BRIAN CEARNES
CREATIVE DIRECTOR
HANNAH BLACKMORE
SENIOR EDITOR
STEPHANIE KISTNER
DESIGNER
JEANNEL CUNANAN
JUNIOR EDITOR
AMANDA LEES
FOOD EDITOR
REBECCA MELI
OPERATIONS MANAGER
DAVID SCOTTO

COVER PHOTOGRAPHER
JAMES MOFFATT
COVER STYLIST
ARUM SHIM

PRINTED IN CHINA
BY C&C OFFSET PRINTING

TITLE: SUPER QUINOA / PAMELA CLARK.
ISBN: 9781742458489 (HARDBACK)
NOTES: INCLUDES INDEX.
SUBJECTS: COOKING (QUINOA)
COOKING (CEREALS). NATURAL FOODS
OTHER CREATORS/CONTRIBUTORS:
CLARK, PAMELA (FOOD DIRECTOR)
DEWEY NUMBER: 641.631

PUBLISHED BY BAUER MEDIA BOOKS,
A DIVISION OF BAUER MEDIA PTY LTD,
54 PARK ST, SYDNEY; GPO BOX 4088,
SYDNEY, NSW 2001, AUSTRALIA
PH +61 2 9282 8618; FAX +61 2 9126 3702
WWW.AWWCOOKBOOKS.COM.AU

ORDER BOOKS
PHONE 136 116 (WITHIN AUSTRALIA)

OR ORDER ONLINE AT
WWW.AWWCOOKBOOKS.COM.AU

SEND RECIPE ENQUIRIES TO
RECIPEENQUIRIES@BAUER-MEDIA.COM.AU